To Signe with love from Ingeborg
Dec. 69

DESIGN   *Shirley Errickson*

COMPOSITION   *Barre Publishers*

PRINTING   *The Meriden Gravure Company*

First printing June 1964
Second printing September 1964
Third printing December 1965

Second Edition January 1968
Second Edition, second printing March 1969

front cover: Lantern on the facade of 53 Beacon Street
against the background of numbers 54 and 55

endpapers: Boston from the Bunker Hill Monument

title page: Bas-relief by John Paramino of the Founding of
Boston Common on tercentenary monument at Beacon and
Spruce Streets

back cover: Iron balconies on 63-64 Beacon Street

BOSTON:

Barre Publishers, Barre, Massachusetts 1964

BOSTON FOUNDED A.D. 1630

Portrait of a City

Photographs by Katharine Knowles

Text by Walter Muir Whitehill

Brewer Fountain and the State House in the spring

BOSTON HILLS *have proved less eternal than those of Rome. Since the Revolution all save one have been reduced or eliminated, trundled down in carts to fill in the coves. The burying ground established in 1660 on the summit of Copp's Hill saved the North End's hill from the general leveling; nobody risked disturbing the rest of the Mathers. Beacon Hill, upon which the State House stands, is but the reduced central summit of the Trimountain, whose lateral peaks have completely disappeared. One could parody the jingle "Ten little Injuns standing in a line", although fortunately it would not continue to the definitive "then there were none." but would stop at two.* ∽ *In the spring of 1958 in a Lowell Institute course entitled* Supra montem posita *I attempted to describe as much of the physical evolution of Boston over three centuries as I could compress into eight lectures. When these were published by the Belknap Press of Harvard University Press the following year as* Boston: A Topographical History, *the 104 illustrations were chosen primarily to explain this process of change. Only a few reproduced anything that is readily recognizable today. While much has been lost in Boston, more that is handsome and consistent has survived than in most American cities.* ∽ *For some years my North Andover neighbor, Miss Katharine Knowles, has been carrying a camera through the streets of Boston in fair weather and foul. Thus she has crystallized some of the ephemeral images that those of us who walk, and do not carry cameras, can only attempt to preserve in our minds. At times she has lived on Beacon Hill; at others she has come in regularly from Essex County. As her beat, so far as Boston sidewalks are concerned, has been similar to mine, she has made permanent many of the fleeting impressions of the city that give me daily pleasure. This is completely Miss Knowles's book. She took the pictures as her keen eyes dictated; she has chosen from many negatives those that to her seemed to achieve a portrait of the city. As she has sold thousands of other peoples' books, includ-*

ing mine, at Lauriat's and at the Harvard Cooperative Society, it seemed high time that she should publish one of her own. ～ *Miss Knowles's photographs have been taken within the original Shawmut peninsula and the filled areas immediately adjacent to it. Except for its omission of the South End,* Boston: Portrait of a City *records the present day appearance of much of the area whose evolution I described.* ～ *In the seventeenth and eighteenth centuries the region around the Old State House, at the intersection of Washington Street (then Cornhill), which led to the Roxbury mainland, and State (then King) Street, which went down to the Long Wharf and the sea, was the heart of Boston. The Common was then a great rural open space on the edge of town, extending to upland fields on the slopes of the Trimountain. When the present State House, designed by Charles Bulfinch, was built on Beacon Hill in the last decade of the eighteenth century, the focus shifted. The slopes of Beacon Hill rapidly became (and have remained) a residential area. Rows of Bulfinch houses (now destroyed) were built along Park and Tremont Streets. The Common gradually evolved from its colonial character of pasture-cum-training-field to that of park. Although it never achieved the formal elegance of the Public Garden, created on filled land west of Charles Street, the Common in 1867 was adorned, by the gift of Gardner Brewer, with a bronze French fountain by Lienard and Moreau, the original of which had been made for the Paris exposition of 1855. Miss Knowles's springtime view of the State House with the silhouette of the Brewer Fountain in the foreground is a reasonable introduction to present-day Boston, for near it the Park Street subway has disgorged Bostonians and visitors since 1897. Although this subway — the oldest in the country — has recently been declared a Registered National Historic Landmark by the National Park Service, it is still the chief entrance to the city from adjacent towns, just as Washington Street was in the colonial period. It is no beauty, but it still works efficiently, and those who use it need never worry about parking their cars.*

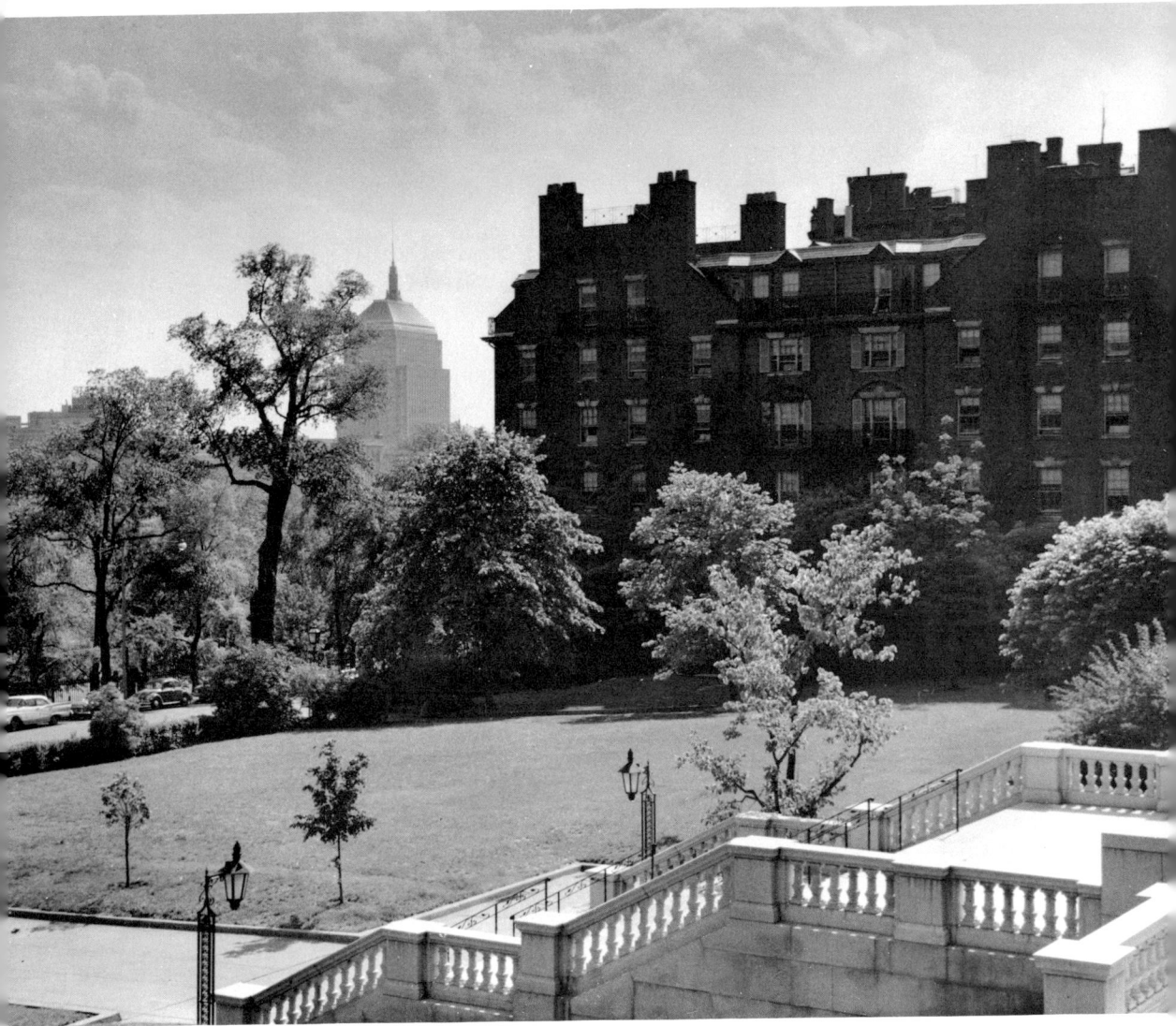

American Unitarian Association from the State House steps

Spring morning in the Public Garden

Miss Knowles has photographed Boston in all seasons. To balance the spring serenity of the Brewer Fountain on page 4, she offers its winter aspect on page 21. Here we have benches in the Public Garden occupied by people enjoying the warm sun. Further on we see the Common on a day when its benches are partially buried in snow. While the contrast of seasons in Louisburg Square is balanced on page 42-43, the arrangement of photographs usually carries on a consistent mood. ∽ The thread upon which the photographs are strung is geographical, but just as a boat changes course to seek favorable winds, so the walker in Boston tacks, backs and fills, for impressions of buildings and vistas. Thus the course of this book is necessarily somewhat circuitous. From the Common and Public Garden, it explores Beacon Hill; proceeds to the Back Bay and Copley Square; thence to Symphony Hall and the museums; through the Fenway to the Charles River basin; back to Park Street; on to the Old State House, Faneuil Hall, the North End, and the waterfront. Here are broad views, small details, buildings, overpasses, water, people of many sorts, that collectively build a portrait of the city as it appears in the seventh decade of the twentieth century.

THE PUBLIC GARDEN *pond, useful for skating in winter and navigation by swan-boat in summer, was created late in 1859. The twenty-four and a quarter acres of the Garden, separated from the Common by Charles Street, and bounded by Beacon, Arlington and Boylston Streets, were the first part of the Back Bay to be turned from water to land. In 1794, to get a clumsy and unsightly nuisance into a remote spot, the town permitted the construction of rope-walks on the mud flats at the foot of the Common. Thirty years later, when the spot was no longer remote, Mayor Josiah Quincy convinced his fellow citizens that this land should be annexed to the Common "and forever kept open and free of buildings of any kind, for the use of the citizens". Although Horace Gray and other private citizens began its conversion into a botanic garden in 1839, planting carefully chosen trees that have now grown to impressive proportions, greedy persons as late as 1850 still hankered to cut it up into building lots.*

The Public Garden pond through willows

opposite: *Artificial and genuine swans in the pond*

An 1859 act of the Legislature, authorizing the filling of the entire Back Bay, established the permanent character of the Public Garden. Soon after its passage, the City government adopted a plan for laying out the Garden, which included the shallow artificial pond, covering three and three-quarters acres, irregular in shape, and complete with island. Its gracefully curving banks offer sites for weeping willows and a Japanese bronze lantern; its waters accommodate not only live swans but

mammoth artificial ones which conceal the man-pedalled pro-
pulsion of the boats upon which generations of children have
circumnavigated the pond. Fifty years ago the men who pedalled
the swan-boats wore the invariable uniform of the choreman of
the day: trousers, waistcoat, shirt with arm garters, stiff collar
(usually without tie), bowler hat, and pipe, (often clay), but
never by any chance a coat. Today, their successors, who look
to me much younger, are often more comfortable in slacks
and sweat shirt.

Every June the southwestern quadrant of the Public Garden is taken over by the tents of the Boston Arts Festival, in which artists of the region show their work. Like every effort to bring contemporary art out of the galleries to a wide audience, the Festival inspires contradictory reactions. The letter columns of the newspapers at this season of the year abound in comments, many of them foolish, for and against the paintings exhibited. It is unfortunate that so few of these critics know of Bliss Perry's

aphorism: "*Very few men and no women write well when they are angry*". The Festival is already a local institution to which thousands come, whether to scoff or pray. It is, moreover, a very cheerful and lively scene, particularly at night when there is music, so pleasant that nobody greatly minds the number of weeks that it takes the grass to recuperate after the removal of the tents. There is the same annual problem in the Harvard Yard when the ten thousand Commencement chairs have been carted away.

As the artificial pond of 1859 imposed a considerable detour upon anyone bound from the Common to Commonwealth Avenue, the City in 1867 spanned it by a bridge, which Mayor Nathaniel B. Shurtleff stated "is esteemed a great ornament and convenience by the frequenters of the Garden". After nearly a century the convenience is taken for granted, but this miniature bridge, suspended over a narrow and shallow artificial pond, is as amiable a conceit as the swan-boats that sail beneath it. Miss Knowles's summer night photograph endows it with a comic opera romanticism.. The scale changes sharply when one looks west across Arlington Street to the Ritz-Carlton Hotel and the John Hancock tower whose weather beacon is useful to anyone who remembers what the colors signify. The Prudential tower, which was hardly above ground when most of the photographs for this book were taken, will, by the time it appears, be the most visible object in the Boston skyline from almost any point in the Back Bay.

Brewer Fountain blanketed in snow

opposite: The State House in winter
following pages: Boston Common in winter

Stormy day on Beacon Street outside the State House

The Curtis Guild steps from Boston Common to Joy and Beacon Streets

Arlington Street Church

Heavy weather at Tremont and Park Streets

Christmas lights and the Park Street Church steeple across the Frog Pond

Boston Common Christmas Crèche at night

BEACON STREET *from Park to Arlington Streets is, like Princes Street in Edinburgh, one-sided, with blocks of rather handsome buildings, looking across Boston Common and the Public Garden. Unlike its Edinburgh counterpart, Beacon Street displays very little for sale, and what there is—books, silver, antiques, cameras, flowers and drugs—is good. Mercifully there is not a single place hawking post cards, souvenirs, or the kind of trash that is manufactured for the tourist trade. ∽ Only a few houses in these blocks are still occupied by private owners in the manner for which they were intended by their builders. Some have been demolished to make way for apartments. In spite of these changes, Beacon Street retains a vestige of its nineteenth century appearance because of the variety of institutions that have taken over dwellings and adapted their interiors to new uses without doing violence to the facades. The American Unitarian Association, the Boston Park Department, the publishing firm of Little, Brown and Company harmoniously share the block between the State House and Joy Street. The Women's City Club, the Somerset Club, and the American Meteorological Association are handsomely and conveniently accommodated in the block between Walnut and Spruce Streets. The Colonial Dames own number 55, which was the residence of the historian William Hickling Prescott from 1844 to 1859. ∽ Brick is the usual material. The fine block west of River Street, illustrated on the opposite page, which was built by the Mount Vernon Proprietors, is of granite, as is the Somerset Club at numbers 42-43, two of whose doorways are illustrated. That club has since 1872 occupied a house built for David Sears by the architect Alexander Parris in 1819, which has been much enlarged. The Greek Revival doorway of number 43, reproduced on page 34, is of the period of the house. The other doorway, with its stout ironwork and formidable lions' heads, which was added in 1872, once led, in spite of its impressive appearance, only to the kitchen. Through subsequent reconstruction it now leads nowhere and thus is never opened.*

61 Beacon Street

opposite: Doorway of 55 Beacon Street
following pages: Doorways of Somerset Club at 43 Beacon Street

THE BOSTON ATHENAEUM, *a proprietary library founded in 1807, has for more than a century occupied substantial quarters at 10½ Beacon Street, diagonally across from the State House. In another city such an address might suggest two rooms upstairs over a meat market; in Boston it has always indicated a spacious and dignified building, occupying frontage appropriate for several whole numbers, whose Italianate sandstone facade would seem entirely at home among the early Victorian clubs in Pall Mall. ⌒ Designed in 1847 by Edward Clarke Cabot, with a sculpture gallery on the first floor, library on the second, and a series of skylighted picture galleries on the third, the building was sympathetically and skilfully enlarged by Henry Forbes Bigelow in 1913. The fourth and fifth floors that he then added blend harmoniously, without slavish copying of earlier details. ⌒ Since the Museum of Fine Arts, incorporated in 1870 as an outgrowth and expansion of the Athenaeum Gallery, moved in 1876 to its own first building in Copley Square, 10½ Beacon Street was devoted entirely to books. It now consists of a series of high rooms, whose alcoves and galleries bring books within easy reach of the reader, and whose windows, overlooking the trees of the Granary Burying Ground, are flooded with morning sun. ⌒ Before the opening of the Boston Public Library in 1854, the Athenaeum was the principal library of the city; in 1850 it also ranked with the Harvard and Yale College Libraries, the Library Company of Philadelphia, and the Library of Congress, as one of the five largest libraries in the United States. With the development of other specialized libraries in the area, the Athenaeum has limited its field to history, literature, and the arts, in which it now has some 430,000 volumes. As it has kept all its early purchases in those fields, and has consistently attempted to add current publications in them, its holdings are more useful for research in the humanities than many college libraries. It has also, as Miss Knowles's photograph of the fifth floor suggests, an inviting atmosphere in which to read.*

BEACON HILL *developed rapidly as a residential area following the building of the State House. In 1795 the Mount Vernon Proprietors bought the property of John Singleton Copley, which covered much of the south slope of the hill, and soon thereafter cut down the west peak of the Trimountain, laying out the present Chestnut, Mount Vernon, and Pinckney Streets parallel to Beacon Street. The original plan for detached houses of generous dimensions, standing in grounds of their own, soon gave way to the familiar rows of red brick houses that are characteristic of the hill today. Louisburg Square, running between Mount Vernon and Pinckney Streets, was gradually built up in the decade following 1834. The north slope of Beacon Hill, between Pinckney and Cambridge Streets, developed more slowly and modestly. Early in the nineteenth century many colored people lived there. Gradually their small wooden houses were incorporated into brick blocks, which were of more modest scale than on the south slope. The little dead-end places leading off Revere Street are the most picturesque streets of Beacon Hill; the tiny houses facing on them are, because of their manageable dimensions, greatly prized. ∽ Chestnut Street west of Charles, once known as Horse-Chestnut Street because of its stables and blacksmiths, now contains apartments, antique and craft shops. The evolution of this region at the foot of the hill is divertingly sketched in Samuel Eliot Morison's* One Boy's Boston. *With the south and north slopes of Beacon Hill, it forms part of the Beacon Hill Historic District, designated in 1963 by the National Park Service as a Registered National Historic Landmark. From Brimmer Street it is an easy transition both in distance and in architectural feeling to the handsome streets of the Back Bay, which present as consistent a showing of Boston domestic architecture of the second half of the nineteenth century as the Beacon Hill Historic District does for the first half. No other city in the United States has preserved such an extensive and consistent group of town houses of the 1860-1900 period as exists in the Back Bay.*

Looking down Pinckney Street from Louisburg Square

Beacon Hill rooftops and the Public Garden from a high Willow Street window

Looking down Mount Vernon Street to the river from the same window

Aristides in Louisburg Square in summer and winter

*Sentry Hill Place (left
and
Bellingham Place
off Revere Street*

A window on Revere Street

opposite: *Window boxes at 105 Myrtle Street*

following pages: *Morning sunlight in Myrtle and Derne Streets behind the State House*

Children in Grove Street wonder what to do

Decorator's shop in Mount Vernon Square

opposite: *A florist's display brightens Charles Street*

opposite: 130 Mount Vernon Street dubbed "Sunflower Castle" by Dr. O. W. Holmes

A late survival plods along Charles Street

opposite: Shops in lower Chestnut Street

Brimmer Street houses and the Church of the Advent

Commonwealth Avenue Mall west of Dartmouth Street

North side of Commonwealth Avenue between Clarendon and Dartmouth Streets

following pages: 6 Commonwealth Avenue (demolished in 1963)
John Hancock tower from the corner of Arlington and Newbury Streets

The Burrage house at Commonwealth Avenue and Hereford Street

The roofs of 315 Dartmouth Street

below: Tower (now wantonly decapitated) of Copley Methodist Episcopal Church with the campanile of the New Old South Church in the background

COPLEY SQUARE *which contains two of the greatest buildings in Boston stumbled into being what it is by accident. In 1871 Trinity Church bought a triangular lot on the east side on which Henry Hobson Richardson designed the great Romanesque building that was the masterpiece of his short career. Within the same decade the Museum of Fine Arts settled on the south side in a building now replaced by the Sheraton-Plaza Hotel, and the Old South Church built on the northwest corner of Boylston and Dartmouth Streets. Then between 1887 and 1895 Charles F. McKim designed his masterpiece, the Boston Public Library, on the west side of the square. Although the library and Trinity Church lend unique distinction to Copley Square, the area has never received the monumental treatment that it deserves. The recent demolition of buildings on the southern corners, through a combination of real estate manipulation and highway construction, has further impaired the setting of these two great monuments. Only the most thoughtful planning can retrieve the damage thus perpetrated; Copley Square deserves this.*

above: Bela L. Pratt's allegorical figure contemplating Copley Square

opposite: Trinity Church against the John Hancock tower

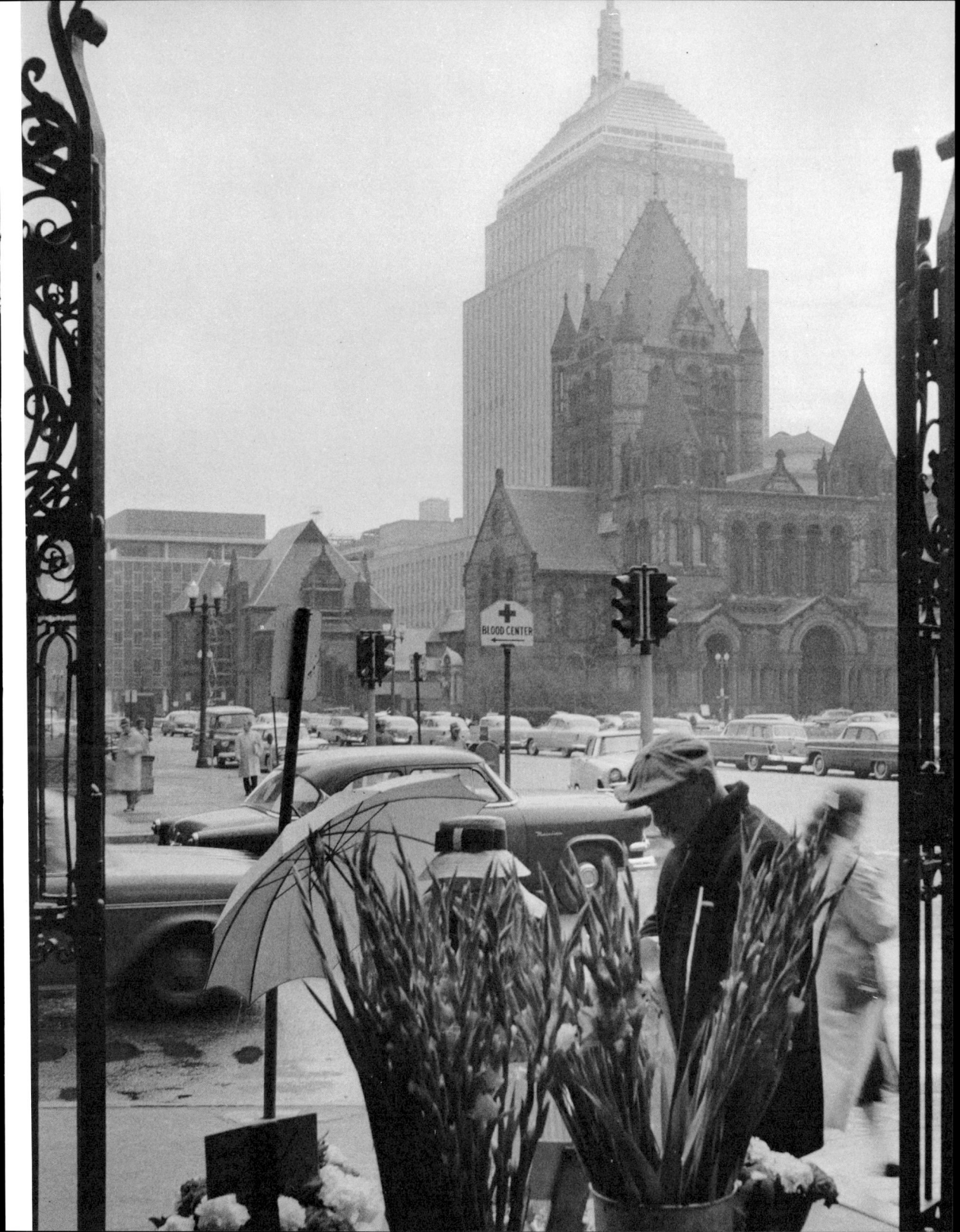

THE BOSTON PUBLIC LIBRARY, *which opened its doors in Mason Street in 1854, was the pioneer in its field. In the United States of today a public library, supported by citizens through their own taxes, is held to be as usual and necessary a part of any established community as a church or a school. So often is this idea taken for granted, it is easy to forget that this institution—the first one of significance—is little more than a century old. ❧ Like all great city libraries, it does much of its best work through branches scattered in all corners of the city, but the central library in Copley Square has an artistic significance that exceeds even the high value of the books that it houses. To me it is the finest building in Boston, and among the greatest examples of nineteenth century architecture in the country. In designing it, McKim took into full consideration its relation to Trinity Church. Severely simple in outline, it is a rectangular granite building, the rear half of which is devoted to book stacks, surrounding an arcaded courtyard. The facade is dominated by the arched windows which light the principal reading room on the second floor, a barrel-vaulted hall 218 feet long, 42 feet wide, and 50 feet high. To the decoration of the library McKim brought painters and sculptors. Puvis de Chavannes did murals for the great stairway, Edwin A. Abbey for the delivery room, John Singer Sargent for a third floor gallery. When the library was opened in 1895 the decorations were still far from complete. As Augustus Saint-Gaudens when he died in 1907 still had not completed the allegorical bronzes that McKim had commissioned to flank the main entrance, the seated figures that appear on pages 62 and 65 were eventually executed by Bela L. Pratt. Over seventy years many adaptations have been made within the building. None are more agreeable than the tent-like pavillions installed in the court to bring books near those who are enjoying the quiet arcades. But some users of the court prefer, as Miss Knowles's picture indicates, to read their own newspapers. When Philip Johnson's addition is built to the rear, McKim's masterpiece, will, I trust, return to its original uncrowded beauty.*

The facade of the Boston Public Library and the New Old South Church

Boston Public Library Courtyard at night

opposite: *A tired shopper reads the news in the courtyard*

HUNTINGTON AVENUE *leads southwest from Copley Square to a great variety of institutions, artistic, musical, scientific, and religious. It passes close to the Mother Church of Christian Science, built in 1894 in Falmouth Street. Due to Mrs. Eddy's express desire that this building be preserved, even when much greater space was required, a vast domed Extension was added to it between 1904 and 1906. The construction of adjacent buildings for the Christian Science Publishing Company, and the conversion of the area between the church and Huntington Avenue into a well-planted park, have done much to alleviate an originally dreary area.* ∽ *From the nineties onward, an increasing number of institutions moved out of central Boston to the westward, where greater space was available. The Boston Symphony Orchestra, founded in 1881, had originally played in the Music Hall at Winter Street and Bumstead Place, a stone's throw from the Common, but in 1893 it began to lay plans to join the westward movement. Thus Symphony Hall, opened on 15 October 1900, was built at the corner of Huntington and Massachusetts Avenues, a short distance beyond the Christian Science Church. As McKim, Mead and White designed a building that, after more than sixty years, still admirably fulfills its musical purpose and is greatly loved, it is unfortunate that it should have been placed in a totally undistinguished location without an inch of ground to spare around it. An underpass carrying Huntington Avenue below Massachusetts Avenue grievously jams the facade. Even before that occurred, most concert goers entered at the side of the hall under the Massachusetts Avenue canopy which offers protection from the weather.* ∽ *Beyond Symphony Hall, Huntington Avenue continues past the New England Conservatory of Music and the rapidly burgeoning Northeastern University to the Museum of Fine Arts, which in 1909 moved here from its first building in Copley Square to gain more spacious surroundings. Thence it continues to the region of the Harvard Medical School and the hospitals that have grown up in its proximity.*

opposite: Christian Science Mother Church and Extension

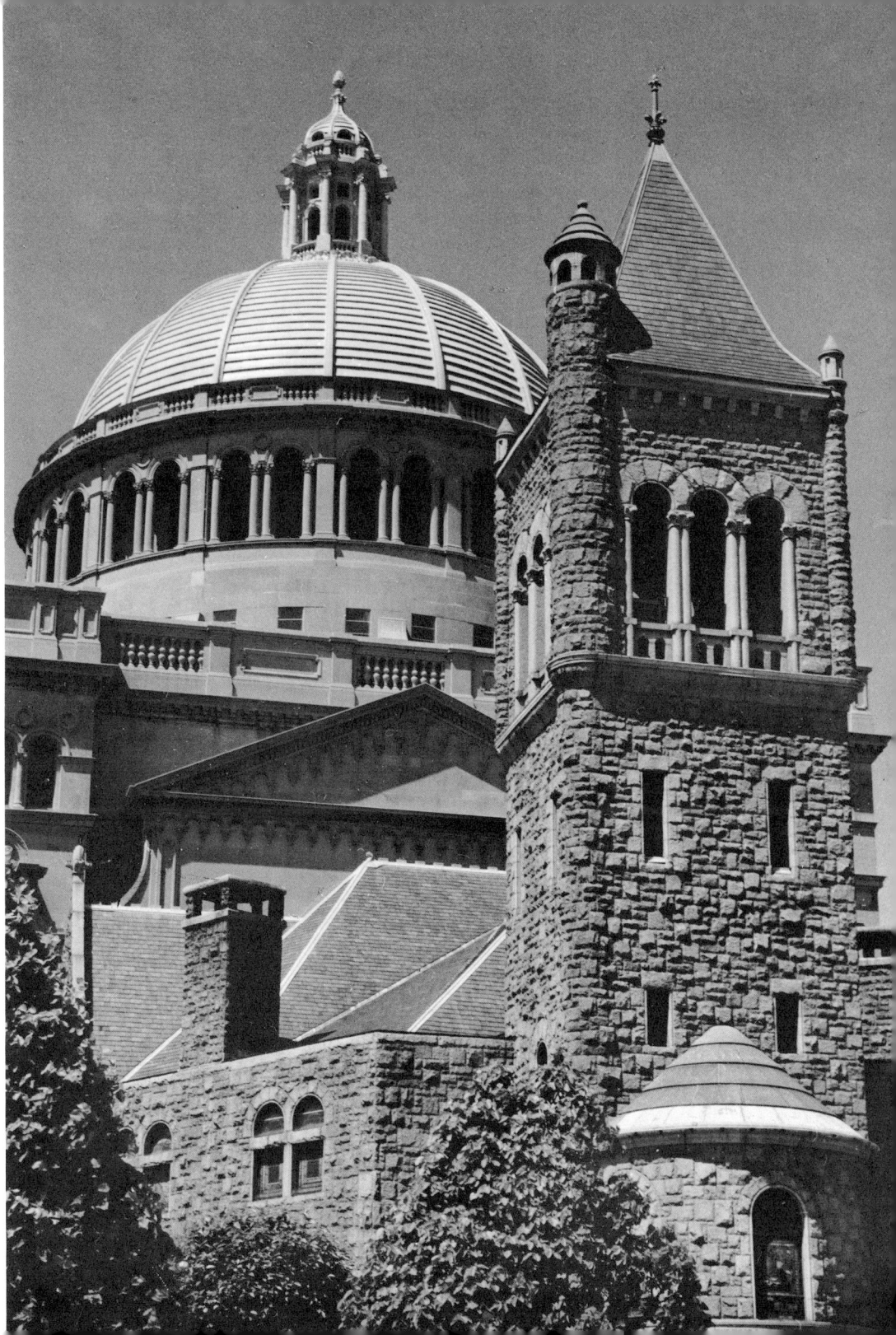

Evening concert time at Symphony Hall

opposite: *Huntington Avenue facade of Symphony Hall*

THE MUSEUM OF FINE ARTS since 1909 has been housed in the granite building in Huntington Avenue, designed by Guy Lowell, whose main entrance appears on the opposite page. From that entrance a great stairway, decorated with murals by John Singer Sargent, leads to a rotunda. To the left one enters the Chinese and Japanese galleries; to the right those devoted to Egypt, Greece, and Rome. Straight ahead a high-studded tapestry hall forms a passageway to the Evans wing, opened in 1915, that contains European and American paintings. Although a decorative arts wing was added in 1928, another section still awaits building to complete the original plan of the museum. ∽ From its incorporation in 1870, the Museum of Fine Arts has been supported entirely by private gifts. The formation of its collections has owed much to the energy and imagination of devoted individuals. The frequent presence in Japan during the last two decades of the nineteenth century of Dr. William Sturgis Bigelow and a group of like-minded Bostonians led to extraordinary acquisitions of Japanese art at the moment when such objects were uniquely available. The Harvard University—Museum of Fine Arts Egyptian Expedition, inaugurated in 1905 under the directorship of Professor George A. Reisner, made major discoveries over decades in Egyptian archaeology and found many of the works of art that now lend distinction to the Museum's collection. The classical department benefited by Edward Perry Warren's intimate knowledge of examples of Greek and Roman art in European private collections and his assiduity in following their appearance in auction sales. ∽ While the Egyptian, classical, and oriental collections are the most remarkable resources of the Museum, constant effort is devoted to the enlargement of the decorative arts and painting collections. Scholars, students, artists, and casual visitors have long been made welcome at the Museum to follow their individual bents. Miss Knowles has summarized this hospitality in the detail from a painting gallery that follows.

ISABELLA STEWART GARDNER, *the wife of the Boston merchant John Lowell Gardner, began collecting paintings in 1888. In the nineties, with aid of the young Bernard Berenson, she raised her sights to such masterpieces as Titian's "Rape of Europa", painted for King Philip II of Spain and later owned by King Charles I of England. In 1899, when her collection had exhausted the space in her two Beacon Street brownstone houses, Mrs. Gardner bought land in the Fenway and began construction of Fenway Court. This great house, incorporating many Italian architectural elements, consists of galleries surrounding a glass-roofed court. Planned from its inception as "The Isabella Stewart Gardner Museum in the Fenway" and formally opened on New Year's night 1903, Fenway Court became a public institution after Mrs. Gardner's death in 1924. Like Sir John Soane in London, she forbade changes, additions, or subtractions to her collection; thus the Isabella Stewart Gardner Museum continues to exhibit its works of art in the setting devised by the collector, and, as such, is a capital monument of taste at the turn of the nineteenth and twentieth centuries. ～ Fenway Court is only a step away from the Evans wing of the Museum of Fine Arts. Both look onto the Fenway, an area converted in the eighties by the genius of Frederick Law Olmsted from the noxious flats of the Muddy River into an enchanting park, where water, grasses, and trees were disposed with oriental subtlety. The Fenway has of late been overrun by automobile traffic; each year some new part is spoiled, but there are still areas accessible only to people and ducks. And it leads to the Charles River Basin, which, since the completion in 1910 of a dam that excluded the harbor tides, has been an attractive body of fresh water. Small boats sail there. In summer symphony concerts are held in the Hatch Shell on its banks at the foot of Chestnut Street. It reflects the buildings of the Massachusetts Institute of Technology and Hugh Stubbins's new apartment house in Beacon Street. It is spanned by the Longfellow Bridge, whose "pepper-pot" towers accent Miss Knowles's night photograph, and which carries the Cambridge subway across the river to Park Street, where she resumes her portrait.*

Courtyard of the Isabella Stewart Gardner Museum

A Fenway pastoral with ducks

opposite: *Looking across the Charles River Basin*

Hugh Stubbins's apartment house at 330 Beacon Street reflected

opposite: *Night symphony at the Hatch Shell*

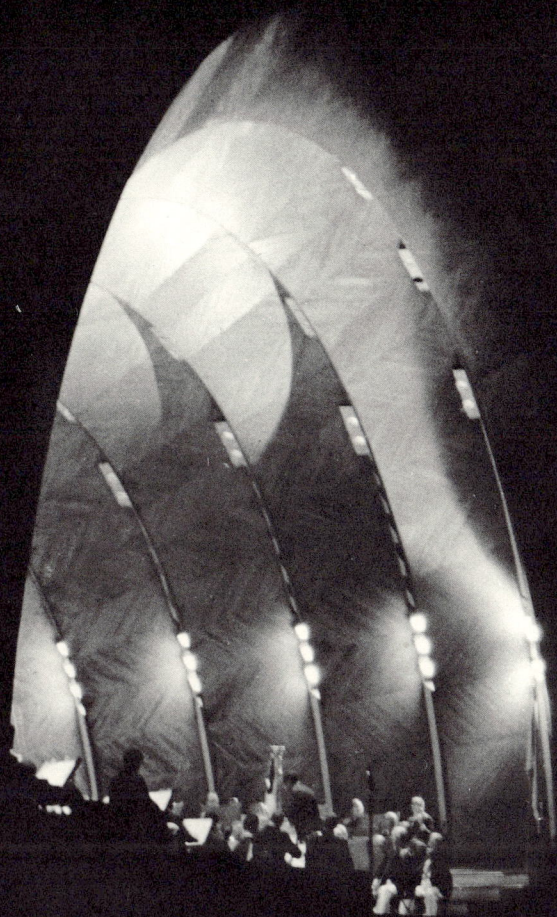

The Prudential tower rises over Back Bay

A young Charles River Basin fisherman

Billowy clouds over the Massachusetts Institute of Technology

Summer reading on the banks of the Charles River Basin

Longfellow Bridge at twilight

opposite: *Platform of the Charles Street Station*

S T . P A U L ' S C A T H E D R A L , *Episcopal, in Tremont Street, was built in 1829 in the Greek Revival style by the architect Alexander Parris, three quarters of a century before the ubiquitous Park Street subway burrowed up entrances practically at its steps. The variety of Boston architecture in the first quarter of the nineteenth century is clearly exemplified at this spot, for from the steps of the Greek temple that is St. Paul's one looks out at Peter Banner's red brick Park Street Church of 1809, whose graceful spire, truncated in the snowy scene on page 27, appears strikingly flood-lit in the night Christmas view across the Common's Frog Pond on the following page. The view of this spire from my office window in the Athenaeum is one of the daily delights of my life. I see it across the Granary Burying Ground, which Miss Knowles has chosen to depict from the ground rather than from my bird's-eye angle. This burying ground, established in 1660, takes its name from the town granary that occupied the site of the Park Street Church in the period when the Common was well beyond the center of Boston and its periphery was the obvious location for odds and ends of municipal institutions. The Granary Burying Ground shelters an extraordinary clutch of revolutionists, John Hancock, Samuel Adams, and Paul Revere among them. Its central pyramid marks the grave of Benjamin Franklin's parents. The presence of these neighbors incidentally gives the Boston Athenaeum and adjacent buildings in Beacon and Park Streets an outlook on grass and trees, unusual in the center of a crowded city.* ～
Just beyond the Granary, King's Chapel, the first Anglican church in the Massachusetts Bay Colony, was built in 1688 in a corner of the earliest burying ground. This was replaced in 1750 by the present church, designed by Peter Harrison. Although the congregation turned Unitarian after the Revolution, the box pews, high pulpit, and sepulchral monuments of Peter Harrison's superb building retain much of the flavor of eighteenth century Tory Anglicanism. Just across the way the Parker House still supplies not only its eponymous rolls, but good broiled tripe, schrod, cod's tongues and cheeks, and other traditional fodder seldom found elsewhere.

St. Paul's Cathedral in Tremont Street

Granary Burying Ground

opposite: *King's Chapel in Tremont Street*

The Oriental Tea Company's great kettle in Court Street

opposite: *The Brattle Book Shop in the Sears Crescent in Cornhill*

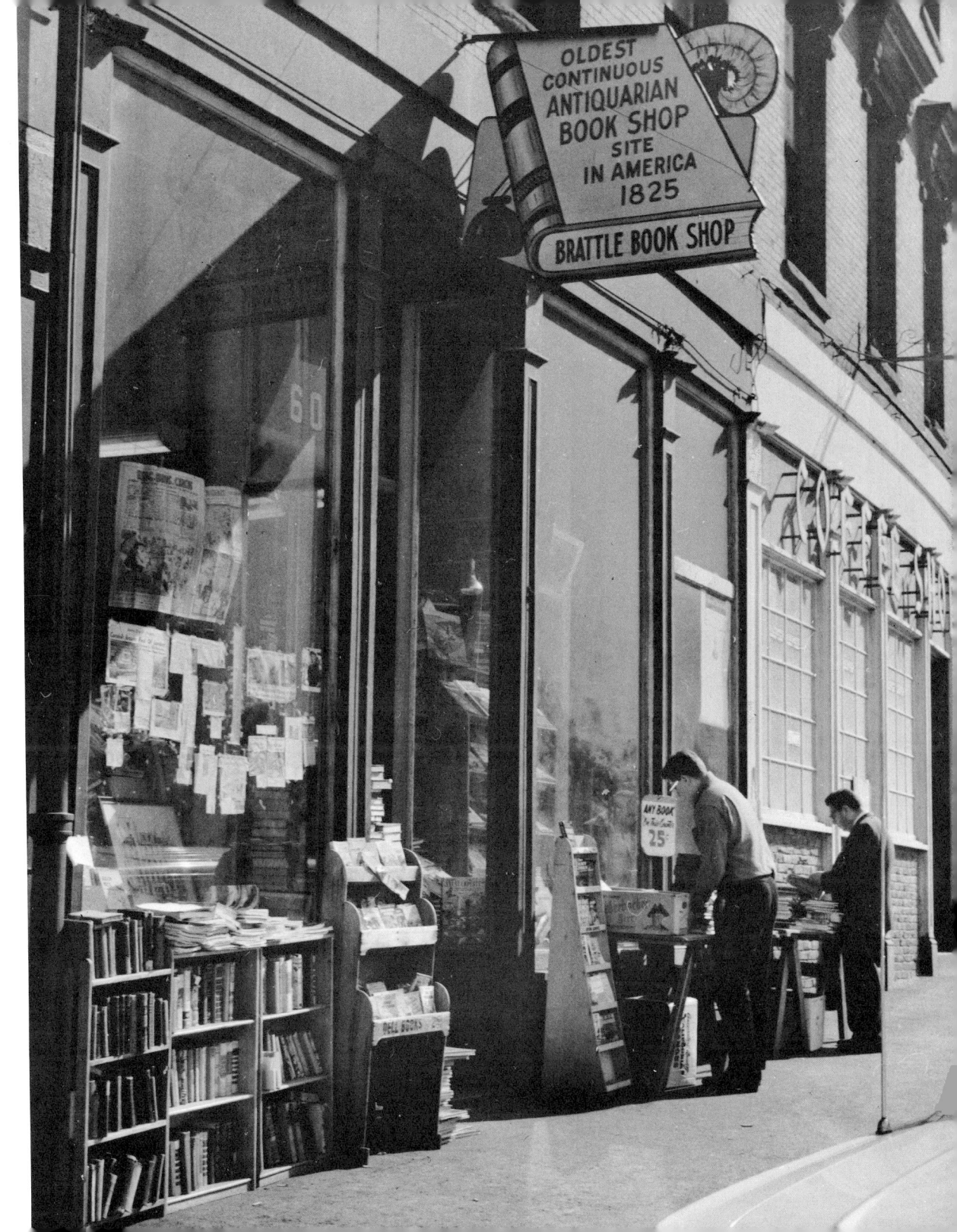

THE OLD STATE HOUSE, *whose (restored) royal lion proclaims its colonial origin, dominated the center of eighteenth century Boston as firmly as the Bulfinch State House does the present city. The transplanted London merchant tailor Robert Keayne, on his death in 1656, left a bequest that led to the building of a wooden Town House on this site, where the chief roads from the sea and the mainland intersected. When Keayne's benevolence was swept away in the great fire of 1711, the town replaced it with a brick structure which housed the town and provincial governments, the courts, and the merchants' exchange. Although this, in turn, was devastated by a 1747 fire, its exterior walls survive in the present Old State House. After the state government moved to Beacon Hill, it served for a time as the town, and then city, hall; fell upon evil days when it was rented out for commercial use, but in 1882 was restored (none too accurately) by the City and made available to the Bostonian Society which maintains a museum of Boston history in it. If the recommendations of the Boston National Historic Sites Commission are adopted by Congress, the National Park Service will soon undertake a better documented restoration of this significant structure. ⌇ From the Old State House it is only a few steps, past the site of the Boston Massacre, to Dock Square, where in 1742 the French Huguenot merchant Peter Faneuil (pronounced locally Funnel, as that is the spelling on his tombstone in the Granary Burying Ground) built the hall which bears his name, which he gave to the town for the use of a market. Originally a two-story building, designed by the painter John Smibert, Faneuil Hall had (as it still has) market stalls on the ground floor, and a sizeable hall for town meetings above. Rebuilt following a fire in 1761 that destroyed all except the brick exterior walls of the 1742 structure, Faneuil Hall was in 1805 enlarged to its present dimensions by Charles Bulfinch, who doubled its width and added a third story, while retaining Smibert's south and east walls unchanged. Although the meetings held in the upstairs hall are no longer as fiery as those pre-Revolutionary ones which earned it the nickname of "Cradle of Liberty, the beef sold in the ground floor market stalls retains its traditional quality.*

FROM FANEUIL HALL *the pedestrian in search of other colonial monuments takes his life in his hand, for the North End is today separated from the rest of the city by a labyrinth of overhead highways, tunnel entrances, and other bedevilments of engineering skill. The North End was very nearly an island, but Hanover Street led straight to it from the center of the town. It no longer does, but anyone who successfully dodges enough cars and finds the right underpass will eventually discover the surviving segment of that street and thereby enter the one part of Boston where people have lived continuously since the earliest settlement. The North End of the nineteen sixties is an extremely sympathetic region, where colonial monuments have acquired congenial Italian neighbors. Its very isolation by the overhead highway gives it the air of a self-sufficient community, with its own shops, restaurants, and religious processions through narrow streets made dazzling by temporary arches of Edison magic. I devoutly hope that the folly of the last decade in obliterating the West End is now so apparent that nobody will dare to tamper with the North End against the will of its inhabitants. ～ The oldest building in the North End is the low-studded wooden house in North Square that was probably built about 1680, but certainly bought by Paul Revere in 1770. Next door is the three-story brick house built by Moses Pierce, glazier, about 1711, and later owned by Nathaniel Hichborn, which, like the Paul Revere House, is preserved as a historic monument. And not far away in Salem Street is Christ Church, built in 1723 for an Anglican parish in the North End, which is the oldest surviving church building in Boston. Although changes in population have deprived it of a natural congregation as completely as if it were a Wren building in the City of London, the Right Reverend William Lawrence and his successors as Bishop of Massachusetts have maintained it as a functioning Episcopal church. The circumstance of Paul Revere having caused signal lanterns to be hung in its steeple, and of H. W. Longfellow having commemmorated that event in verse, have made Christ Church known to millions of Americans and have tagged it with the nickname "Old North Church".*

The M. T. A. on the Charlestown-Forest Hills run

opposite: The North End across a concrete barrier

People of the North End sun themselves

The Custom House tower rising above the expressway that separates the North End from the rest of Boston

Paul Revere's statue points to the tower where his signal lanterns hung

opposite: *Revere's house in North Square*

opposite: *Christ Church in Salem Street*

Details of the now destroyed West End

THE BOSTON WATERFRONT *of today is a ghost of its former self, although not lacking in picturesqueness nor the salt air and smell of fish that are (to the New Englander at least) so pleasing. John Josselyn in 1663 described Boston houses as "for the most part raised on the Sea-banks and wharfed out with great industry and cost, many of them standing upon piles". This process of "wharfing-out" during the two centuries after Josselyn's visit, combined with the practice of cutting down the hills to fill in the coves, pushed the original shore line well into the harbor. The details of this process are the theme of my* Boston: A Topographical History, *but the results can clearly be seen on the opposite page. In that photograph, looking landward from the present wharf line, one sees only in the distant background the tower of the Custom House, whose site in the seventeenth century was well out in the middle of the Town Cove. As the ships have vanished, a number of wharf warehouses have been converted into apartments. Although the ramshackle buildings on T Wharf no longer provide picturesque and economical living quarters, as they did until recently, other more substantial and architecturally distinguished wharf warehouses continue to house occupants who are stalwart enough to consider the admirable view of the harbor as compensation for the icy winds that blow in from sea in winter.* ⌇ *Today's waterfront, like the present shoreline, is a nineteenth and twentieth century creation. The chief link with the eighteenth century is the U.S.S.* Constitution, *built in 1797 but still in commission in the United States Navy, which is berthed at the Boston Naval Shipyard in Charlestown. As one approaches Boston from the Mystic River Bridge, the masts of the venerable frigate and the graceful spire of Christ Church in the North End stand in unforgettable relation to each other. To the left one looks down the harbor toward the sea; to the right is the Charles River Basin; ahead are the towers, steadily increasing in number, that futilely attempt to convert Boston into a two-for-a-cent Manhattan. But if one cannot come in over the Mystic River Bridge, or is too lazy to climb the Bunker Hill Monument, Miss Knowles's end papers for this book are a good substitute.*

Fishing boats at T Wharf

opposite: *Steps that once led to the Blue Ship Tea Room on T Wharf*

A detail of U.S.S. Constitution

U.S.S. Constitution

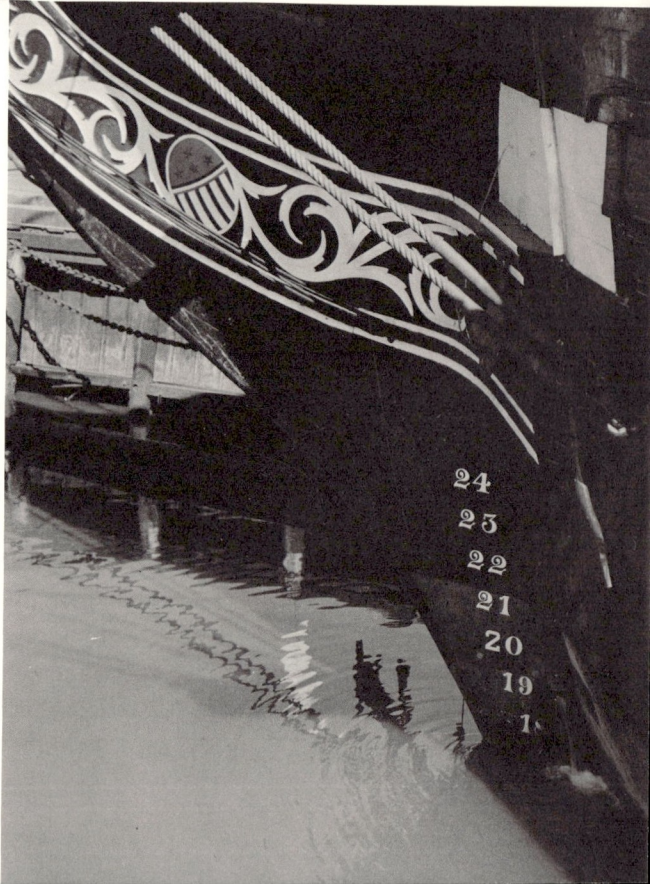